SAINT JOI

TO The
Bishop of Roooome
Have a
Great Christmas
Love from

mum :)

X X

2014

X X

BISHOP DONAL MURRAY

Saint John XXIII
Pope of Vatican II

VERITAS

First published 2014 by
Veritas Publications
7–8 Lower Abbey Street
Dublin 1
publications@veritas.ie
www.veritas.ie

ISBN 978 1 84730 557 2

10 9 8 7 6 5 4 3 2 1

A catalogue record for this book is available
from the British Library.

Cover design by Lir Mac Cárthaigh, Veritas Publications
Cover image: Vatican City, Rome, Italy, May 1963: Profile portrait of
Pope John XXIII.
© Bettmann/CORBIS
Printed in the Republic of Ireland by Hudson Killeen Ltd, Dublin

*Veritas books are printed on paper made from the wood pulp
of managed forests. For every tree felled, at least one tree is planted,
thereby renewing natural resources.*

CONTENTS

INTRODUCTION

Sotto il Monte, which means 'at the foot of the mountain', is a small village in the province of Bergamo in northern Italy. An entry in its baptismal register reads:

> In the year 1881, 25 November, I, Francesco Rebuzzini, the priest of this parish church of St John the Baptist of Sotto il Monte, baptised the infant born today of the lawfully married couple, Giovanni Battista Roncalli and Marianna Mazzolla, from Brusico in this parish. The infant was given the names Angelo Giuseppe. The godfather was Zaverio Roncalli, the son of Giovanni Battista of this parish.[1]

Angelo Giuseppe Roncalli was the fourth child in a family of tenant farmers. There were fourteen children

---

[1] Cf. John XXIII, *Journal of a Soul* (London: Chapman, 1965), p. 409.

altogether, but the wider family included his father's cousin and his children. The total household was nearer to thirty. Although he left home at the age of eleven to begin his studies for the priesthood, he remained close to his family throughout his life.

The family and neighbours who saw him growing up could never have dreamed that, in his honour, the official name of the village would become Sotto il Monte Giovanni XXIII.

PREPARING FOR PRIESTHOOD

Angelo Roncalli's early schooling took place in the diocesan seminary of Bergamo. While there he kept a journal which records the rules he set himself for becoming a good priest and for growing closer to the Lord. This was published after his death as *Journal of a Soul*. There are entries from 1895 to some months before his death in 1963. These writings were intended for his own use and, at least in the beginning, he never dreamt that they would be a historical record:

> The portrait that emerges is of a serious-minded, intense, painfully scrupulous adolescent, tempted only by gossip and *gourmandise*.[2]

But one also sees in the journal as he grew older a remarkably perceptive mind and an ability to reflect with

---

[2] P. Hebblethwaite, *John XXIII* (London: Geoffrey Chapman, 1984), p. 16.

great honesty on himself, his life and on the political and social issues of the time.

In 1900 he won a scholarship to study in Rome. Among his professors was one who believed that Church history was a centrally important but often neglected subject in seminaries. Whether that was the reason or not, Roncalli showed a particular interest in Church history throughout his life. Towards the end of the following year his studies were interrupted by a year of military service which he found to be 'a real purgatory'.[3]

He was awarded a doctorate in theology in the Lateran University. Part of the examination leading to that award was set by Monsignor Eugenio Pacelli, who, as Pius XII, would be his immediate predecessor as pope.[4]

---

[3] *Journal of a Soul*, p. 333.
[4] M. O'Carroll, *Pope John XXIII* (Dublin: Golden Eagle Books, 1959), p. 21.

BISHOP'S SECRETARY

On 10 August 1904, Angelo Roncalli was ordained a priest. The following day he said his first Mass and was introduced to the recently elected Pope Pius X, who promised 'to ask the Lord to bless these good intentions of yours'.[5]

Giacomo Radini-Tedeschi was appointed to the Diocese of Bergamo as its new bishop. That marked the end of formal studies in Church history for young Fr Roncalli; he was chosen to be the bishop's secretary.

The new bishop was able and determined; he undertook his task with great energy. There were divisions among the clergy dating back to the previous bishops. This gave the new secretary the opportunity to hone the diplomatic skills which would serve him well in later life. He accompanied the bishop on his visits to parishes in the

---

[5] *Journal of a Soul*, p. 162.

diocese, and worked with him to awaken awareness of social needs. Among the initiatives of the bishop were the summoning of a diocesan synod which decided on the founding of a religious congregation, for diocesan priests to assist the bishop in carrying out particular ministries like pastoral care of schools and the giving of retreats. Father Roncalli joined this new congregation, called Priests of the Sacred Heart.

War broke out in August 1914. Pope Pius X died a couple of weeks later. Then the Bishop of Bergamo died after less than ten years in office, aged only fifty-seven. His secretary used his historical background to write an extensive biography, called simply *My Bishop*.

The life of this bishop's secretary changed dramatically. Soon he was back in the army, first in the medical corps and later as a chaplain. After the war he worked in a student hostel and then spent some years in Rome in the Congregation of Propaganda Fide (for the spreading of the faith). His particular role was to build up a missionary sense in Italy. The idea that a missionary spirit should exist in every part of the Church, not just 'on the missions', was to be one of the key ideas of the Council that he was to call.

THE DIPLOMAT

The next big step in his life was a considerable shock to him. On 19 March 1925, he was ordained titular Archbishop of Areopolis and appointed as papal representative in Bulgaria. His assignment was a difficult one. Catholics comprised a very small minority in a country that was overwhelmingly orthodox, with a considerable Muslim population. He spent almost ten years there, and such was his love for the country that he asked the pope to change his titular see to Mesembria, now called Nesebar, an ancient diocese on the Black Sea coast of the country. He described it as 'a veritable jewel of Bulgaria'.[6]

The next assignment was in Istanbul as Apostolic Delegate to Turkey and Greece. Once again he was living in predominantly Muslim countries, and once again the situation was very complex. The Catholics were of many

---

[6] *John XXIII*, p. 142.

nationalities – French, Italians, Austrians – and of many different rites – Maronites, Melkites, Chaldeans and so on. Most of the Christians were Orthodox, and Istanbul was the home of the Patriarch of Constantinople, the first among the Orthodox Patriarchs. In his first homily in this delicate situation one can hear a foreshadowing of the welcoming tones of Pope John and, indeed, of Pope Francis:

> In Jesus' Church there are not first- and second-class citizens. All peoples are invited equally to sit down at the same banquet of heavenly doctrine and to share in the life of grace that saves, sanctifies and rejoices the heart.[7]

During his ten years in Istanbul, Turkey was being transformed into a secular state. It remained neutral for almost the whole of World War II. Archbishop Roncalli had to deal with issues of extraordinary delicacy: 'the proximity of the explosive Middle East, the passage of diplomats from the European Catholic powers, the interests of the major contestants in Turkey.'[8]

Another move came in December 1944 when he was appointed Apostolic Nuncio to France. This too was not an easy post. There was deep anger against the politicians

---

[7] *John XXIII*, p. 144.
[8] *Pope John XXIII*, p. 43.

and other leaders who were blamed for the national humiliation of the fall of France. The new government was seeking the removal of something like twenty-five bishops who were accused of co-operating with the Vichy government. There was an element of scapegoating involved in this. Some of the accused bishops had protested vigorously in favour of the Jews and against Nazi atrocities. These questions were ultimately decided by Rome with a small number of bishops eventually resigning. In all of these matters, the influence of the Nuncio's friendly and simple manner was fruitful:

> The Nuncio's method was to show affability and kindness to everyone, to give hospitality in the largest handed way and to use humour and wit to the maximums compatible with the dignity of his office.[9]

In an address to the European Parliament in 2013, President Michael D. Higgins spoke of a meeting attended by Archbishop Roncalli in Luxeuil-Les Bains in July 1950. The occasion was the celebration of the 1,400th anniversary of the birth of St Columbanus. The meeting, however, was 'organised to facilitate a meeting of Robert Schuman, Foreign Minister of France, with like-minded

---

[9] *Pope John XXIII*, p. 55.

others ... to hear and test his great idea for the coming together of the countries of Europe'.[10] Those present included Archbishop (later Cardinal) Feltin of Paris, Archbishop McQuaid of Dublin, the Bishops Kyne of Meath and O'Neill of Limerick, the Taoiseach John A. Costello, the Minister for Foreign Affairs Sean McBride and the Leader of the Opposition, Eamon de Valera. Columbanus is buried in Bobbio, about 160 kilometres from Sotto il Monte. The Nuncio spoke of the place of the saint in the history of Europe, calling him 'the living expression of fourteen centuries of light'.[11]

[10] M. D. Higgins, 'Towards a European Union of the Citizens', Strasbourg, 17 April 2013.
[11] *Pope John XXIII*, p. 60.

PATRIARCH OF VENICE

At the end of November 1952, Archbishop Roncalli learned that he was to be made a cardinal. On 12 January 1953 he received the red hat and was appointed Patriarch of Venice. The boy from Sotto il Monte returned to his native Italy with an extraordinary wealth of experience. He had spent ten years intimately involved in the life of his native diocese. He had spent time in Rome studying and then working with students. He had been involved in fostering a missionary spirit in Italy. He had spent twenty years in Muslim countries which brought him into contact with the Islamic world. It also involved close contact with the Orthodox Churches as well as with Oriental Churches in union with Rome. He had spent ten years in France in the aftermath of World War II. Perhaps the only common factor was that every change brought new and unexpected challenges.

At seventy-one, he must have assumed that this was his last appointment. It was again marked by his affability and approachability with priests and laity. The political situation of the time was complex with the rise of Communist and Socialist influence and many tensions as to how the Christian Democrats and the Church should react to this new challenge. The patriarch sought to temper extreme positions on both sides and to calm those in Rome who were looking for action that might have exacerbated the situation.

In his final year as patriarch two events are of interest. He was papal legate at the ceremonies in Lourdes on 25 March 1958 for the opening of the underground basilica of Pius X. There was a sense of coming full circle as he consecrated the huge church dedicated to the man who blessed him on the day of his first Mass and whom he called 'the pope of our youth'.

On 27 December 1958, he ordained Albino Luciani as Bishop of Vittoria Veneto. Bishop Luciani would later be his successor as Patriarch of Venice and as the short-lived Pope John Paul I.

POPE

Since his arrival in Venice there had been suggestions that he might be *papabile*. As time passed, however, it seemed that he was too old to be considered. He was in his seventy-seventh year.[12] At that time, the last pope elected in his seventies, as far as can be ascertained, was Clement XII in 1730.

Nevertheless, on the eleventh ballot of the conclave he was elected. The world, and perhaps the cardinals, thought that he would be a 'transitional pope' whose task would be to keep things 'ticking over' until a suitable younger candidate would emerge. If so, they were mistaken! The pontificate was to be a short one of just over four and half years, but it was not uneventful.

The choice of the name John was the first of many surprises. It was a choice made by someone who valued his roots: it was his father's name and the name of his

---

[12] The same age at which Pope Francis was elected.

native parish. It was a sign that he took seriously his role as Bishop of Rome, because, as he pointed out, 'it is the name of our cathedral',[13] the Lateran Basilica. But perhaps most significantly it was the choice of a historian. The name John had fallen into disuse as a papal name, not least because of doubt about the legitimacy of the last man to have claimed the title. The new pope resolved for the conclave the dilemma about what number should be attached to the name:

> It is the name that has been most used in the long series of Roman pontiffs. Indeed there have been twenty-two unquestionably legitimate supreme pontiffs named John.[14]

His open and friendly relationship with those of other faiths is summed up in an incident which made a deep impression on Jonathan Sacks, former Chief Rabbi of Great Britain and the Commonwealth:

> Meeting a delegation of Jews in 1960, he [Pope John XXIII] said, in the words of the Bible itself, 'I am Joseph your brother'. That, both in the biblical

---

[13] Quoted by Hebblethwaite, p. 286, from *Vent'Anni*, Rome 1978, edited by Pope John's own secretary, Loris Capovilla, who was named a cardinal in the constistory of February 2014, at the age of ninety-eight.

[14] The pope's second baptismal name was Guiseppe, meaning Joseph.

original and its recent reenactment, was an extraordinary scene of reconciliation.[15]

Only three months after his election, John XXIII announced to a group of seventeen cardinals his intention to summon an ecumenical council. This was to be the defining event of his papacy. It marked the beginning of a renewal which was transitional in a sense completely different from what was expected!

[15] J. Sacks, 'On Creative Minorities', Erasmus Lecture, New York, 31 October 2013.

THE COUNCIL

The Council required several years of preparation. The first session opened on 11 October 1962. Numbered among those present was the young Fr Joseph Ratzinger, who was to become Pope Benedict XVI. He described the pope's opening address as one of the positive aspects that appeared 'even in the opening ceremony':

> ... he disavowed all merely negative condemnation and asked instead that the Council apply the medicine of compassion. The Council was not to engage in scholastic disputation, arguing the points of specific doctrines. Rather their efforts were to be directed toward a fundamental renewal of the universal Church, in living dialogue with the present time and its needs.[16]

---

[16] J. Ratzinger, *Theological Highlights of Vatican II* (New Jersey: Paulist Press 1966), p. 22.

In that opening address of the Council, Pope John XXIII disagreed with those who, 'though fired with commendable zeal', take a pessimistic view of events. He called them 'prophets of doom' and once again the historian in him spoke: 'One would think from their attitude that history, that great teacher of life, had taught them nothing.'[17] Down the centuries, he said, various errors have arisen and 'often vanished as quickly as they came, like mist before the sun':

> The Church has always opposed these errors, and often condemned them with the utmost severity. Today, however, Christ's Bride prefers the balm of mercy to the arm of severity. She believes that present needs are best served by explaining more fully the purport of her doctrines, rather than by publishing condemnations.[18]

Once again, one can see some of the approaches that we have come to associate with Pope Francis. A small but telling incident during the first session is worth recording. On 10 November, Bishop Cule of Mostar repeated a request that several bishops had already made, asking that

---

[17] Opening Address to the Council, 11 October 1962 (http://www.vatican.va/holy_father/john_paul_ii/speeches/1979/october/documents/hf_jp-ii_spe_19791001_maynooth-religious-people_en.html).
[18] Ibid.

the name of St Joseph be inserted in the Eucharistic Prayer. He spoke somewhat repetitively and was abruptly cut off by the presiding cardinal. This bishop had been imprisoned and suffered greatly under the Communist regime in Yugoslavia. Three days later, Pope John, who had been following the debate, and who knew Bishop Cule and his heroic history, issued a decree inserting the name of Joseph as the bishop had requested.[19]

---

[19] J. A. Komonchak, https://www.commonwealmagazine.org/blog/st-joseph-canon-mass; cf. X. Rynne, *Vatican Council II* (New York: Orbis Books, 1999), pp. 75, 76.

ENCYCLICALS

Remarkably, in less than five years he wrote eight encyclicals. Two of these are particularly significant. In May 1961 he produced *Mater et Magistra*, Mother and Teacher. It was published on the seventieth anniversary of the publication of *Rerum Novarum* by Leo XIII in 1891.

One of those who suggested such an encyclical was Fr Joseph Cardijn, founder of the Young Christian Workers Movement. Cardijn's method of social analysis – See, Judge, Act – was strongly endorsed in the encyclical.[20] At a time of rapid change the encyclical focused on the core of social teaching – the dignity and rights of every member of the human family:

> ... the economic prosperity of a nation is not so much its total assets in terms of wealth and

---

[20] Cf. *Mater et Magistra*, 236, 237. Joseph Cardijn was named a cardinal in 1965, before the end of the Council.

property, as the equitable division and distribution of this wealth.[21]

In late 1962 the world came terrifyingly close to nuclear war, and Pope John broadcast an eloquent appeal for peace. Some months later he published *Pacem in Terris*, Peace on Earth. The openness of John XXIII is expressed in what might seem a small detail – this was the first encyclical ever to be addressed not just to bishops, clergy and Catholic faithful but to all people of good will. Pope Francis summed up the message and the challenge of Pope John's vision of the foundation of peace:

> … it consists in the divine origin of man, of society and of authority itself which calls individuals, families, different social groups and States to live out relations of justice and solidarity. It is the duty of all men and women to build peace following the example of Jesus Christ, through these two paths: promoting and exercising justice with truth and love; everyone contributing, according to his means, to integral human development following the logic of solidarity. Looking at our current reality, I ask myself if we have understood the lesson of *Pacem in Terris*? I ask myself if the words

---

[21] Ibid., 73, 74.

justice and solidarity are only in our dictionary or if we all work so that they become a reality?[22]

The encyclical was published on 11 April 1963. Less than two months later he succumbed to cancer. He had been informed of the diagnosis about three weeks before the Council opened. He hoped that the work of the Council might be over after one session and that he might preside over the completion of what he had begun. It was not to be. But it was he who called the Council and set its tone and its aims. It is his great legacy. The young man from the little village who developed an interest in Church history played no small part in that history. No doubt, his little village will become known as Sotto il Monte *San Giovanni XXIII.*

[22] Address to Conference Celebrating the 50th Anniversary of *Pacem in Terris,* 3 October 2013.